THE PRODIGAL

THE PRODIGAL

DEREK WALCOTT

FARRAR, STRAUS AND GIROUX

New York

Farrar, Straus and Giroux
19 Union Square West, New York 10003

Distributed in Canada by Douglas & McIntyre Ltd.
Printed in the United States of America
First edition, 2004

Portions of this book appeared in *American Poetry Review*, *The New Yorker*,
Poetry, and *The Times Literary Supplement*.

Library of Congress Cataloging-in-Publication Data
Walcott, Derek.
The prodigal / Derek Walcott.— 1st ed.
    p.   cm.
ISBN-13: 978-0-374-23743-1
ISBN-10: 0-374-23743-3 (hc : alk. paper)
    1. Saint Lucia—Poetry.   2. Greenwich Village (New York,
N.Y.)—Poetry.   3. West Indians—Foreign countries—Poetry.
4. Europe—Poetry.   5. Exiles—Poetry.   I. Title.

PR9272.9.W3P76 2004
811'.54—dc22

                                         2004005147

Designed by Gretchen Achilles

www.fsgbooks.com

1   3   5   7   9   10   8   6   4   2

TO LUIGI SAMPIETRO

PART I

1

I

In autumn, on the train to Pennsylvania,
he placed his book face-down on the sunlit seat
and it began to move. Metre established,
carried on calm parallels, he preferred to read
the paragraphs, the gliding blocks of stanzas
framed by the widening windows—
Italian light on the factories, October's
motley in Jersey, wild fans of trees, the blue
metallic Hudson, and in the turning aureate afternoon,
dusk on rose brickwork as if it were Siena.

Nothing. Nobody at the small railroad station.
The willows fan open. Here we hung our harps,
as the river slid past to elegiac banjos
and the barge crawled along an ochre canal
past the white spires of autumnal towns
and racketing freight trains all long whoop and echo.
Stations, bridges and tunnels enter their language
and the scribble of brown twigs on a blank sky.

And now the cars began to fill with pilgrims,
while the book slept. With others in the car,
he felt as if he had become a tunnel

through which they entered the idea of America—
familiar mantling through the tunnel's skin.
It was still unfamiliar, the staidness of trains.
And the thoughtful, the separate, gliding in cars
on arrowing rails serenely, each gripped face intent
on the puzzle of distance, as stations pass
without waving, and sad, approaching cities,
announced by the prologue of ramshackle yards
and toothless tunnels, and the foliage rusting
across an old aqueduct, loomed and then dwindled
into their name. There were no stations
or receding platforms in the maps of childhood
nor blizzards of dogwood, no piercing steeples
from buttressed cathedrals, nor statues whose base
held dolphins, blunt browed, repeating themselves.
Look at that man looking from the stalled window—
he contains many absences. He has ridden
over infinite bridges, some with roofs below,
many where the afternoon glittered like mica
on the empty river. There was no time
to fall in love with Florence, to completely understand
Wilmington or the rusty stanchions
that flashed past with their cables
or how the screaming gulls knew
the names of all the women he had lost.
There was sweet meditation on a train
even of certain griefs, a gliding time
on the levelled surface of elegiac earth
more than the immortal motion of a blue bay
next to the stone sails of graves, his growing loss.

Echoing railway stations drew him to fiction,
their web of schedules, incoherent announcements,
the terror of missing his train, and because trains
(their casual accuracy, the joy in their gliding power)
had (there were no trains on the islands
of his young manhood) a child's delight in motion,
the lines and parallels and smoky arches
of unread famous novels would stay the same
for yet another fall with its bright counties,
he knew, through the gliding window, the trees would lift
in lament for all the leaves of the unread books,
Anna Karenina, for the long wail of smoke
across Alpine meadows, for soldiers leaning
out of war-crowded stations, a separate joy
more rooted in landscapes than the flare of battles.

In the middle of the nineteenth century,
somewhere between Balzac and Lautréamont,
a little farther on than Baudelaire Station
where bead-eyed Verlaine sat, my train broke down,
and has been stuck there since. When I got off
I found that I had missed the Twentieth Century.
I studied those small things which besieged the station,
the comical belligerence of dragonflies
and the perpetual astonishment of owls.
It was another country whose time had passed,
with pastoral willows and a belief in drawing.
I saw where Courbet lived; I saw the big quarry
and the lemon light of Jean-Baptiste Camille Corot.
The noise of roaring parliaments, a noise
that sounded like the ocean, whorled in my ear-shell,

was far, and the one sibilance was of the poplars
who once bowed to Hobbema. My joy was stuck.
The small station was empty in the afternoon,
as it had been on the trip to Philadelphia.
I sipped the long delight of a past time
where ambition was too late. My craft was stuck.
My deep delight lay in being dated
like the archaic engine. Peace was immense.
But Time passed differently than it did on water.

II

There is a continent outside my window,
in the Hudson's patient narrative. There's some calm.
But traffic hurtles up the West Side Highway,
and in fall, the embankment blazes, but
even in spring sunlight I have rarely sought
the glittering consolation of the river,
its far-fetched history, the tongues of unknown trees
talk to an old man sitting on a bench.
Along the smouldering autumnal sidewalks,
the secretive coffee-shops, bright flower stalls,
wandering the Village in search of another subject
other than yourself, it is yourself you meet.
An old man remembering white-headed mountains.
And subtly the sense insinuates itself
that frequent exile turns into treachery,
missing the seasons at the table of July
on lower Seventh Avenue when young women glide
like Nereids in their lissome summer dresses,

all those Susannas for a single elder!
In spring the leaves sing round a tireless statue
who will not sit although invited to.

From a fresh- to a salt-water muse. Home to the Hudson.
The bells on a bright Sunday from my bed,
the squares of sunlight on the buildings opposite
the river slate, the sky cloudless, enamelled.
Then Sunday brings its summary of the world,
with the serene Hudson and its criss-crossing ferries,
great clouds and a red barge.
Gaze, graze on the numinous greys
of the river, its spectral traffic
and the ghostly bridges, the bouquet of lamps,
along the embankment your name fades into fog.

Clouds, the sag of old towels, sodden in grey windows,
the far shore scumbled by the fog,
ducks bob on the grey river like decoys,
not ducks but the submerged pieces of an old pier,
lights fade from the water, "Such, such were the joys,"
muffled remorse in the December air.

III

Desire and disease commingling,
commingling, the white hair and the white page
with the fear of white sight, blindness, amputation,
a recurring kidney stone, the plague of AIDS,
shaken in the mirror by that bewildered look,

the truculence, the drooping lip of a spiritual lout.
Look at it any way you like, it's an old man's book
whenever you write it, whenever it comes out,
the age in your armpits in the pleats of your crotch,
the faded perfumes of cherished conversations,
and the toilet gurgling its eclogues, resurrecting names
in its hoarse swivelling into an echo after.
This is the music of memory, water.

IV

On Mondays, Boston classes. Lunch, a Korean corner—
my glasses clouded by a tribal broth,
a soup that tamed shaggy Mongolian horsemen
in steaming tents while their mares stamped the snow.
Asia swirls in a blizzard; winter is rising
on drifts across the pavements, soon every gutter
will be a locked rivulet then it will be time
for rose and orange lights to dot the Prudential,
and sparrows to bulb along the stricken branches.
I missed the fall. It went with a sudden flare
and blew its wick in Gloucester, sank in Salem,
and bleached the salt grass bending off Cape Ann,
flipped seals into the sound, rattled the shades
of a dark house on that headland abandoned
except by Hopper. You know the light I mean.
American light. And the wind is
the sound of an age going out the window,
yellow and red as taxis, the leaves. And then
boring through volumes of cloud, a silverfish—

2

I

Chasms and fissures of the vertiginous Alps
through the plane window, meadows of snow
on powdery precipices, the cantons of cumuli
grumbling or closing, gasping falls of light
a steady and serene white-knuckled horror
of speckled white serrations, inconceivable
in repetition, spumy avalanches
of forgetting cloud, in the wrong heaven—
a paradise of ice and camouflage
of speeding seraphs' shadows down its slopes
under the metal, featherless wings, the noise
a violation of that pre-primal silence
white and without thought, my fear was white
and my belief obliterated—a black stroke
on a primed canvas, everything was white,
white was the colour of nothing, not the night,
my faith was strapped in. It could go no higher.
I doubted that there would be a blest descent
braking like threshing seraph's wings, to spire
and sun-shot field, wide, innocent.

The worst fear widened, to ask of the infinite:
How many more cathedral-spires? How many more

peaks of these ice-seized mountains, and towns
locked in by avalanches with their yellow lights
inside on their brilliant goods, with the clappers
of bells frozen by silence? How many small crows
like commas punctuating the drifts?
Infinite and repetitive as the ridges
patterned like okapi or jaguar, their white forests
are an opposite absolute world, a different life,
but more like a different death. The wanderer's cry
forms an O of terror but muted by the slanted snow
and a fear that is farther than panic. This,
whatever its lesson, is the tacit chorus
of the screaming mountains, the feathering alp,
the frozen ocean of oceanic roofs
above which hangs the white ogling horn—
skeletal tusk of a mastodon above white inns.

II

A small room, brown and dark, its linen
white as the white spur of the Matterhorn
above the balcony and the dark inns in snow,
and, incredibly on the scars of the crevasses,
a train crawling up the mountain. Orange lights
and brighter in the muffled streets of Zermatt,
what element more absolute as itself
than the death-hush of the snow, the voiceless blizzard,
between the brilliant windows of the stores?

He stood outside bright windows filled with music,
faint conversation through the mullioned panes
and crab-clenched chandeliers with pointed flames
above the animate and inanimate faces
of apparitions whose features matched their names,
all gentlemen with some big-buttressed dames,
a fiction in a fiction. The door could open,
he would be more than welcome. The lights were squared
on the lawn's edges. A conspiring pen
had brought him thus far. All that he had dared
lay in elegant ambush whose bright noise
was like the starlit surf whose voice had reared
him. But this was a different climate,
a different country. Now both lives had met
in this achievement. He turned his head
away this time, and walked back towards the road.
The scene was just like something he had read.
Something in boyhood, before he went abroad.
But cowardice called to him. He went back inside;
secure and rigid in their printed places
all of the dancers in that frozen ballroom.

III

As with snow, to feel the air changing,
the heart darken and in the clarity of sunshine—
the clarity of ice, as in the islands,
all spring, all summer, it was the one world
till autumn marshalled its divisions, its flags,
and deer marched with agreeing nodding antlers

into another fiction while we remained
in immortal cobalt, unchanging viridian;
and what was altered was something more profound
than geography, it was the self. It was vocabulary.
Now it was time for the white poem of winter,
when icicles lock the great bronze horse's teeth.
The streets were white. No sidewalks in the streets
and the short snowy distances between the shops
brilliant with winter gear and above the streets
full of skiers with their poles on their shoulders
the chalets, snow-roofed, with peaks like Christmas cards.
From a climate without wolves, what if I dreamt
a white wolf trotted and stood in my path,
there, in the early lights of the busy streets
thickened to silence, coal-eyed, its tongue
a panting flame, snow swarming my eyes.
Then, like a match struck with light! A different glow
than the windows of the hotels, the stores, the inns.
Her hair above the crisp snow of table linen
was like a flare, it led him, stumbling, inane.

He went down early to the lounge. Repeat:
He went down early to the lounge and waited.
The street lights were still on. Then they went out.
Eventually she came and when she came,
she brought the mountain with her into the big room
with her cold cheeks, snow smudged with strawberries,
her body steaming with hues of a banked hearth,
her eyes the blue-green of its dying coals,
and her hair, once it was shaken from its cap
leapt like new fire. Ilse, perhaps, brought in

the muddy tracks between the inns, dark pines,
the unicorn shaft or the priapic horn
of the white mountain, as famous as its stamp,
she brought in echoes of hunted stags folding
from a shot's ricochet through a crevasse
in the warmth of the body which she now unsheathed,
shaking the dust of snow from fur and leather
and hanging her ski-coat on a rack of antlers,
with a glance that pierced him like an icicle,
flashing the blizzard of white teeth, then tousling
the wet hair at the nape of her neck, she stood
for a moment in a blizzard of linen
and the far-lightning flash of cutlery
over the chalets and lodges of Zermatt.

IV

As far as secular angels go there is always one,
in Venice, in Milan, hardening that horn
of ageing desire and its devastations,
while skiers plunge and slide soundlessly
past crevasses, invisible as thoughts,
like the waitress buttoning her uniform
already pronged by an invisible horn
and lids that sometimes closed as if her form
slept in the white peace after an avalanche.
He looked out through the window at white air,
and there, crawling impossibly like an insect
across the drifts, a train, distinct, impossible.
Now with more promise than he could expect.

Her speech was crisp, and as for the flushed face,
was it a patronizing kindness? Who could tell?
Auf Wiedersehen to the pines and the peaked chalets
to the inns looking like toys behind the car
and the waitresses and Ilse, indifferently
going about their business with the lamps
of the Alpine dusk, and the beds freshly made
as the new snow that blurred the villages
and the lights from the stores on the banked street
and the receding shore of our hotel.
Again, how many farewells and greetings
on cheeks that change their name, how many kisses
near tinkling earrings that fade like carriage bells.

V

On the powdery ridges of the slopes were sheds
where cattle were byred in the winter darkness.
I imagined them blindly gurgitating their fodder,
and beyond them the vertiginous fissures
in the iron cold. There were the absolute,
these peaks, the pitch of temperature and terror,
polar rigidities that magnetized a child
these rocks bearded with icicles, crevasses
from Andersen's "Ice Maiden," Whittier's "Snow-Bound,"
this empire, this infernity of ice.
One afternoon, an eternity ago
in his warm island childhood in a jalousied room
with all the fire of daylight outside
in the bustling, black, barefoot street, his heart

was iced with terror, a frozen pond, in which
glazed faces started behind the glacial prose
of Hans Christian Andersen's "The Ice Maiden"
with its snow-locked horror, and that
afternoon has never left me. I did not know then that
she worked as a blond waitress in Zermatt.

I liked the precocious lamps in the evening.
I had never seen so much snow. It whitened night.
Out of this snow, like weeds that have survived,
came an assiduous fiction, one that the inns,
the gables shelved with white, the muted trails,
and (unavoidable) the sharp horn of the peak,
demanded of the ritual silence, a flare of light,
the flush of a warmed face, some elegy,
some cold enchantress, an ember's memory
of fire, provided since my young manhood
or earlier, of the Ice Maiden. She and the horn
were from the same white magic and when she came,
she lifted her head and the horn hooked my heart,
and the world magnified a greeting into love.

Wide meadows shot with a lemon light under the peaks,
the mineral glint of distant towns, the line of the plain
ending in the exclamation of a belfry!
Entering Lausanne, after the white ridges,
ochre scarps for a long while along the grey lake,
a lake so wide you could not see the other shore,
nor if souls walked along it, arms outstretched.
So many of them now on the other bank!

Then the old gentlemen at lunch in Lausanne
with suits of flawless cut, impeccable manners,
update of Rembrandt's *Syndics of the Drapers' Guild.*
I translated the pink, shaven faces of the Guild
to their dark-panelled and polished ancestry
of John the Baptist heads each borne on a saucer
of white lace, the loaded eyes, the thinning hair
over the white streaks of the foreheads, a syndicate
in which, far back, a negligible ancestor
might have been a member, greeting me
a product of his empire's miscegenation
in old Saint Martin. I could find no trace.
Built in huge gilt frames I sometimes found myself
loitering among the markets and canals;
but in Geneva though I felt hung and mounted
in sepia rooms with a glazed stare.
Immense and grey, with its invisible shore.
The weather sounded like its name: Lausanne.
Thought furred and felt like an alderman's collar,
a chocolate stick for the voracious fog.

Irradiating outwards from that grey lake,
that grey which is the hue of historical peace
Geneva was the colour of a statesman's hair,
silvery and elegant and with a statesman's conscience,
banks and furled flags above the banks, and shoes
mirrored and quiet in deep-piled carpets.
The velvet, soft transactions of the world.
Stipple of farmhouse and fields, foothills dissolving
to lilac, violet shadows in the ridged furrows,
a spire slowly spinning away into Italy.

3

I

Blessed are the small farms conjugating Horace,
and the olive trees as twisted as Ovid's syntax,
Virgilian twilight on the hides of cattle
and the small turreted castles on the Tuscan slopes.
To live in another language with the swallow's wings:
chelidon beating over the rye, shadows on the barley,
between the peeling farms and the rusted poplars,
the bright air full of drunken insects,
the Pervigilium Veneris, Latin words leaping to life
as the train glides into dividing Florence.

Outside Firenze the hill offered itself,
erect-flame cypresses and an ochre castle
sepulchral towards evening, a star's first spark,
over the red-brown tiles of roofs through the olive grove,
dusk delicate as an old gentleman
with mottled hands and watery eyes, our host.
Diabetic, dying, my double.
And here again, a digit in Rome's bustle—
"Rome's bustle," a phrase as casual as a cape
tossed over the shoulder of a dimming pilgrim
in an obscure, anonymous altar-piece.

Those serene soft mountains, those tacit gorges—
that was Abruzzi. I remembered Abruzzi
from A Farewell to Arms, with the soft young priest
who invites Frederic Henry there after the war,
and perhaps Frederic Henry got there, whether or not,
here it was now, with small hill towns on the ridges,
where it could be infernally cold. The precise light
defined bright quarries. It looked incorruptible
as the faith of a young priest. Its paint still wet.
It spun past, saying, "You swore not to forget
fighting and the rattle of gunfire in the mountains."
Gone, without echo: Only the tight fine towns,
church tower or spire, the steep rust roofs
revolving slowly past the carriage window.

We drove through the wet sunlight into Pescara.
Wind folded the deckchairs on the esplanade,
slamming them shut. A detached, striped umbrella
somersaulted over the sand. A dishrag sky.
Then the weak sunshine strengthened steadily
and colour came back into the sea's face.
The waitress moved among the afternoon tables
setting and straightening the dinner linen;
a girl with jet hair, black as her skirt, red mouth
and cheeks that were brightening now with the sun
and the drying sand. The sky grew Caribbean.
The breakers chumbling in from the Adriatic,
the folded beach umbrellas like a Chinese army
waiting for the drop of their Emperor's sword.
Through the dirty glass of the hotel in Pescara
a mixture of spume and grime, a quiet

like an armistice, the clink, like small weapons, of cutlery,
the rumours darkening like smoke over Albania,
the palms on the sea-front ceaselessly tossing,
the traffic with slow headlights inching through rain.
And O it was lovely coming through the mountains,
castles on the far crests, the flashing olives
and the halted infantry of the pines. All the wars
were over or far away. But the young woman on the bus
past whose beauty the pines, the olives and the small castles swept
in the clarified window, and whose sadness I thought
was like a holiday resort-town in the rain,
the lights of her grey eyes like glistening traffic
whose name, she told me, was a mountain flower's
but one that was quite common in her country,
spoke softly as the drizzle on Pescara's shore-front
of Serbia and its sorrow, of the horrors she had seen
on the sidewalks of Kosovo, and how it was, all war,
the fault of the Jews. Yet she said it with calm eyes.
I learnt this later. I learnt it from the drizzle
and the car lights of Pescara lancing the dark
and the folded umbrellas, quiet as banners
of the long brown hair that bracketed her face.
Leon. Yehuda. Joseph. The war was their fault.
But it was lovely coming through the mountains
that they said were the Apennines when I asked their names.

II

The tidal motion of refugees, not the flight of wild geese,
the faces in freight cars, haggard and coal-eyed,

particularly the peaked stare of children,
the huge bundles crossing bridges, axles creaking
as if joints and bones were audible, the dark stain
spreading on maps whose shapes dissolve their frontiers
the way that corpses melt in a lime-pit or
the bright mulch of autumn is trampled into mud,
and the smoke of a cypress signals Sachsenhausen,
those without trains, without mules or horses,
those who have the rocking chair and the sewing machine
heaped on a human cart, a waggon without horses
for horses have long since galloped out of their field
back to the mythology of mercy, back to the cone
of the orange steeple piercing clouds over the lindens
and the stone bells of Sunday over the cobbles,
those who rest their hands on the sides of the carts
as if they were the flanks of mules, and the women
with flint faces, with glazed cheekbones, with eyes
the colour of duck-ponds glazed over with ice,
for whom the year has only one season, one sky:
that of the rooks flapping like torn umbrellas,
all have been reduced into a common language,
the homeless, the province-less, to the incredible memory
of apples and clean streams, and the sound of milk
filling the summer churns, where are you from,
what was your district, I know that lake, I know the beer,
and its inns, I believed in its mountains,
now there is a monstrous map that is called Nowhere
and that is where we're all headed, behind it
there is a view called the Province of Mercy,
where the only government is that of the apples
and the only army the wide banners of barley

and its farms are simple, and that is the vision
that narrows in the irises and the dying
and the tired whom we leave in ditches
before they stiffen and their brows go cold
as the stones that have broken our shoes,
as the clouds that grow ashen so quickly after dawn
over palm and poplar, in the deceitful sunrise
of this, your new century.

III

O Serbian sibyl, prophetess
peering between your curtains of brown hair
(or these parentheses), if I were a Jew,
you'd see me shuffling on the cobblestones
of some unpronounceable city, you could watch
my body crumble, like the long, trembling ash
of a cigarette in the hand of a scholar
in a sidewalk restaurant, you beauty
who had the name of a common mountain flower
that hides in a cleft of the rocks
on the white-haired ridges of Albania.

IV

Among ragged palms and pastel balconies,
this miracle also happened in Pescara,
by accident, or by coincident stars.
In the hotel lobby of a forgotten name

as mine will be forgotten by another, I
who was reading a paperback of the life of Nora,
J. Joyce's wife, from which there is now a film,
with a photo of the actress on the cover,
a film at the film festival in that city
with its furrowed bay by a long esplanade,
met the black-haired Irish beauty playing her
and told her that and I showed her the book
to our mutual astonishment, also her friend's
another young Irishwoman with red hair,
her beauty's guardian, I guessed, and I made
of this something more; oracular
and fated, although all it meant
was that we were both here at the festival,
but it was more. Perhaps. I liked to believe
that she was Nora, and not that I was Joyce,
but to be reading the paper with her picture
in the basic, salty furniture of the lobby
while the seaside light made her skin manifest
with Irishness, with none of Nora's fairness
but with her accent, seemed to me a miracle
of which as evidence of that epiphany
while the rain stopped on the shining esplanade,
I have in her warm hand untouched by fame,
like the scrawl of seaweed on unprinted strand,
the lilting whisper of her signature.

4

I

O Genoan, I come as the last line of where you began,
to the port whose wharf holds long shadows and silence,
under the weeds of the prow, nodding and riding with
the wavering map of America. Droplets of oil
conjugate themselves into rainbows, the greased rag
blurs the portholes and the moorings sway
until Genoa glides past, a fog of spires
absorbing the gull's return. Hands close like wings
in the aisles of the cathedral. The palms close
and the psalms and the choir's O
widens and deepens in the wave's trough,
in the interminable metronome, grave and cradle,
until over the crest there is a fresher crest,
against preliminary reefs, the surf's exploding light!
Lice sing in the timber and the sponges open.

Seaside hotels with their salt balconies
whose iron flowers rust with artifice
facing the pompous, cavernous railway station
utilitarian monument of the Fascists;
down the serrated summer coast from Nice
to Genoa, the sea's tinfoil striations
are close to home. The cedar's agitation

repeats the rustling of reversible almonds,
the cheek warmed by a freshly ironed sky;
scent of scorched grass, and, through the limp leaves—
the Mediterranean doing its laundry.
Then somewhere, from the window of your eye,
a flag lifts a corner of the afternoon,
as an iron swarm of Vespas hurtles by
and the Discoverer's statue fades round the turn.
All these remembered women melt into one,
when my small words, like sails, must leave their haven:
the cliffs of shoulders burnt brown by the sun,
and wild jet hair, the banner of the raven.

In Genoa I loved our balcony. Below me,
the white stone statue of the Admiral
. kept quiet in the navigating traffic,
the open gate to the Mediterranean, the sea—
with the same swell that heaved the caravel's sigh
at the remorseful future that lay ahead—
in the stone-flagged park close to the railway station.
Conglomerate masonry, shaft-light on brick
in the old Quarter, squeaking pulleys
lifting the sails of laundry across the gulf
of inconsolable alleys, the pigeon's dandruff
powdering the hair and shoulders of creased statues
who forget what they were famous for—
the whitewashed Admiral also. There is no rest for
the insomnia of sculptures, the snow's nightmare,
the smell of history I carry in my clothes
like smoke, the smell of a washed street in Pescara,
the sun-on-stone smell of the hills of Tuscany,

flowers in the weed between the rocks, wild flowers
the train passing their hosannas on the slopes,
and the soul, in exile, sliding into its station—
into History, the Muse of shutters and cabinets,
past the closed cathedral of the gramophone.

II

Envy of statues; this is how it grew:
every day in Milan, en route to class,
I passed my rigid, immortal friend, the General,
on his morose green horse, still there on weekends.
The wars were over but he would not dismount.
Had he died, catapulted in some charge
in some euphonious battle? The bronze charger
was lathered, streaked with sweat, in the summer sun.
We had no such memorials on the island.
Our only cavalry were the charging waves,
pluming with spume, and tossing plunging necks.
Who knows what war he fought in and whose shot
tumbled his whinnying steed? Envy of fountains.
Poor hero on his island in the swirl of traffic,
denied the solace of an umbrageous linden
or chestnut with bright medals through its leaves.
Envy of columns. Calm. Envy of bells.
Peace widened the Sunday avenue in Milan.

Left-handed light at morning on the square,
the Duomo with long shadows where clamouring bells
shake exaltation from blue, virginal air,

squaring off corners, de Chirico parallels—
and where the soundlessly snorting, big-balled horse
whose head, lowered and drooping, means the death
of its rider, holds a far longer breath, longer
than ours in our traffic island.
The widening love of Italy growing stronger
against my will with sunlight in Milan . . .
For we still expect presences, no matter where—
to sit again at a table watching the luminous clatter
of the great mall in Milan; there! was that him,
Joseph in an olive raincoat, like a leaf
on a clear stream with a crowd of leaves
from the edge to the centre and sinking into them?

III

Absence's emblem, the solid spectre of your grief,
yes, you can still see his tonsure, his ascetic halo,
till somewhere bars it, a hat or a sign, then
the mall fills with phantoms serenely hurrying
to the same exit the arched doorways of a sunlight
almost celestial, I silently shout their names
but I am inaudible, to them, since they outnumber me,
to them I am the phantom and they are the real ones,
their names still claiming them over the noise
of waiters clearing the tables of their possessions,
of the crumbs of bread and the glasses of recent blood
still clouded with their one breath, the breath
that I too will leave in a water-glass to condense
when I join them following the pale tonsure

of a moon that fades into the glare of the dawn
outside the intricate and immense cathedral
and our terrestrial traffic; the changing light.
Within the circumference of the cathedral
and its immense and bustling piazza
and a long mall of cafés and shops, I saw him,
because I needed to; because a lengthening absence
requires its apparition, lost, then returned again
by the frothing crowd, I was not ready
for the stone-webbed and incantation-hallowed
intricacies of the altars, an architecture
like frozen fury, demanding a surrendering awe.

IV

I wanted to be able to write: "There is nothing like it,
to walk down the Via Veneto before sunrise."
And now, you think: he is going to describe it.
I am going to describe the benediction of June,
the grey cool spring air, its edges at *prima luce*,
too early for coffee from the hotel
and from the locked grids of last night's cafés,
the dew as wet as Pescara's the year before,
and the canvas umbrellas folded in their scabbards,
the reason being the difference in travel-time,
the difference being the night clerk yawning at the end
of his vigil, and the surly, early waiter,
then the long, unechoing empty street
that isn't as quiet as he had imagined,
with traffic building, the spiky palms

outside the American Embassy and two policemen
because of the threat of terrorists, the huge trees
against the pale buildings, the banks and arches
with their dirty flags; the lights still on
on certain buildings as the widening light
palely washed their facades, but the stillness
exactly like Gros Ilet's, the sea and the village,
if not the vermilion buses under the trees
their lights still on, there, here it comes, the light
out of pearl, out of Piero della Francesca,
(you could tell he would mention a painter),
then slowly the whole fresco with the spring's gold
on Ministerio del Lavoro e delle Politiche Sociali
at whose gate a man came out and examined me
as I copied the name down, a bald young man
in an orange windbreaker who scowled
because of my colour and the terrorists,
and because my village was unimportantly beautiful
unlike his city and the Via Veneto,
its curved facades gamboge and ochre, grey stone,
the unnamed trees forming a gentle tunnel
over the buses, their lamps now out, vermilion, orange,
and what was missing was the smell of the sea
in the early morning on the small embankment,
but the palms as still in the dawn's docile tissue
Bus No. 63 L 90 Pugliese
whereas no echo in the name Gros Ilet,
no literature, no history, at least until now.
Bus 116, lights on. On the Via Veneto.
Glides, like a fish, softly, or a turning leaf.

I lived in two villages: Greenwich and Gros Ilet,
and loved both almost equally. One had the sea,
grey morning light along the waking water,
the other a great river, and if they asked
what country I was from I'd say, "The light
of that tree-lined sunrise down the Via Veneto."

5

I

You did not venture far from your hotel.
Prodigal, in your untethered pilgrimage,
your shadow was your tutor and your guide;
your gaze was as immediate and real
as a concrete culvert or a plate-glass store
and the crowd, contemporary and simply urgent,
looked at every city through a filter
of dishevelled sepia sketches, visual echoes,
arches and washerwomen by an ex-aqueduct,
Corot or Guardi, your shadow was a footnote
in some boulevard's infinite paragraph
with names, fountains and plaques—
from the glittering linen tables set before dinner
there came the memory of this afternoon sea,
creased, but as blinding. Fog blurred the windows,
and a canal minted its coins. My heart
was available for a reasonable price.
The waiters rubbing glasses like the fog.
All seemed to know this. They avoided my eyes.
They were very preoccupied. The lights came on.
Petals were lit down the long boulevards.
As an orange disk drops in the violet sea

that a canoe crosses as the candles bud
in their glass cases, your shadow grows enormous.

Come down the hotel stairs into Montale,
come past the balustrade into Machado,
let Quevedo be in the red cushions in the foyer
and Goya in the false gold of the picture-frames
and outside, in the separations of sunlight,
stand by yourself, unreal in either world.
Since, perhaps soon, these pages must be closed,
forgive us our treacheries, so lightly lost!

The Alps receding in the blue irises
of Ilse, the water folding itself in braids
behind Roberta's hair in the Grand Canal,
the startled eyebrows of gentle Esperanza
like sparrows lifting from the cobbles in Alcalá,
and astonished aqueducts, and breakfast linen.
We read, we travel, we become.
To enter class was like entering a gallery;
instead of walls of institutional concrete
set every head against a painted vault
with every hair alert with smoothness, place Laura's
with heavy-lidded, stone-grey eyes, brown Isabella's
with the tan of a wild wood-nymph, imagine
the lids of Leda closing for the rattle of the swan's wings,
like Isabella's, the older one, set Roberta's
lips parted in perpetual annunciation,
and give each one her painter, her appointment.

All of those beauties, Paola, Sandra, Roberta,
are centuries old; they have inherited the silks,
taffeta and precious stones, the smoothed velvet
of heavy eyelids and the golden furze
along a forearm, immortal models
of those framed miracles of portraiture
and their invisible strokes, this one
with the Botticellian cheekbones, that one
with the gaze of the ferret-stroking girl
by Leonardo, and she of the seamless brow
of plaster by the master from Urbino,
as if each in turn had stepped down from a wall
through an arched doorway into an ageless light
enlivened by the wind in blouse and jeans.
Still there were some irreconcilable things,
such as an implacable lust that came with age—
as a dirty old man leering at young things
in the name of their common, aye common, craft,
an old white egret beating priapic wings
from a sunlit stand of reeds to a still pond,
the pivot of its slowly widening rings.
Irises in which I am never found.

II

It is only afterwards that these things are ours:
An aria, then a piano, practising scales.
A stab in the heart, the cheese-coloured walls
of Parma, the small square, the opera-house,
and the walls of stone farmhouses gliding past us

on some immortal Sunday, and the hay rolled up in bales
between the long poplars and the sun-dried pastures
and the furled umbrellas of the cypresses,
scenes ending in soft nods, in silent yesses.
Complete possession. And Europe?
Surrender it as the waves render the idea
of opera and the ochre walls of Parma;
or flags long fluttering on the Boulevard du N'importe Quoi,
or the gate in a hedge that opens into England,
or let it claim what's half, at least, its own
from illegitimate or legitimate blood,
a Shylock muttering among the canals
or the gilded Moor, from the harp-shaped willows
on the oily canals of Amsterdam
and that white house between the German lindens
that folded your spectre like an envelope,
or if, carried on a black charger of starched lace,
a young blackamoor brought in my ancestor's head
to the orange-fleshed burghers of the Drapers' Guild
at that luncheon in Lausanne.

III

After the museums and the sunlit streets,
and after the awning with its uniformed porters
and the excessive solicitude of the concierge,
in all that completion there is still an emptiness,
for all the trees and shadows outside the Prado,
an emptiness that is echoed in the soft eyes
of the surrendering general at Breda.

This lesson was bequeathed me by Velázquez
in the casual sanctity of the Prado—
there is its nadir, *The Surrender of Breda*—
in the defeated general's face, its creased smile,
the damp gaze with such compassion for the victor
before the yielding tilt of the lances—
a gentle ecstasy, a mortal sweetness,
the deeper truth of failure, deeper than triumph.
In concentration on the strokes of a face,
a creased musician shaking a shac-shac,
the flesh not flesh but khaki, all afternoon
reworking the frown, the wrinkles, in country delight
but your small gift fading over the hills, receding,
and your own eyes acquiring the surrender
of a brush or a sword or a pen reversed
before the tilted lances in the dusk of despair.
In your ambitious, pompous panel of a country fete,
work on those minuscule extra figures. They too have lives.
Meanwhile, on the high corner of the fresco, look—
on some obscure hill, with the size of beetles,
their pincers with the far ferocity of lances
their shield, their armour catching the golden dusk
another battle is waging its own business,
inaudible and tiny, negligible;
those little figures, their separate narrative
away from but parallel to the centre
where the monumental clangour is in progress
or rather in its postural, hieratic stasis.

We fill the same perspective, Mantegna, Uccello, Signorelli,
in the central mass and meaning of the world,

in the sunlit margins with our little states,
our insect anger, our tiny flags and lances.
These are not yours, by either inheritance—
all the great vaults, the populous rotundas,
gigantic saints in their arrested rhetoric,
in the riven sky, the fabric the sky-bolt sunders
in the unending exodus of the Flood.

IV

Pray for the depiction of taffeta
how it proceeds from softness to softness,
rustling pliancy, the holes in lace,
instead, an awkwardness that is close to laughter,
or the eye leaves it too quickly, its disgrace,
requiring more and more strength, more and more prayer,
pray at the border of the sweetness of despair—
its obscure grace.
Cotton-wool hair and a mahogany face.
What does it take? You know what it must take.
It takes three hundred years.
No. Go back further, to Cimabue and Crivelli,
to a frieze of announcing angels with gold-crusted nimbuses.
Today it will either totter into life,
stagger and erect itself, as a calf its own easel,
in the level morning light, today it will smell
grass and dung and the foam, wild around the rocks,
or again it will be stillborn,
cotton-wool hair and mahogany face.
And no smile of encouragement from della Francesca,

from Velázquez, from Vermeer, from grouching Degas.
Even the white foam, dead.
And what is that symbol of the sword reversed,
the pen, or pencil, their magic staff returned,
but your own soul to Europe, to the stirring lindens
and bent chimney smoke? Conquest and debt.
The muttering grey canals of Amsterdam.

Narrative originates in the heart, time's
pendulum and apostrophe, until the heart's scales
are swung to a standstill, to a breathing balance,
a light meridian of the hemispheres—
saying to the sea and Europe, "Here I am,"
division swayed by justice, poetry
unbiased to an absolute pivot, that is my sword's
surrendering victory over myself, my better halves.

6

I

To go to Germany for the beautiful phrase
unter den Linden, which, like a branch in sunshine,
means "without History, under the linden trees,"
without the broken crucifixes of swastikas,
with the swathe of summer, green hillocks and red roofs,
through rusted pines, the village of her girlhood,
of braids and chocolate, and yet there is guilt
in all that green. Still, History is healing,
and charity is its scar, its carapace.
They do not live in life, they inhabit their fiction,
those with names like novels, especially the Russians
who had the narrow faces of academic drawings
whose features concealed intractable sorrow
so that, since they were fiction, their deaths were okay
and the dust powdering their streets and the massacres
that would grow famous and look for an index
in which they could be shelved; after all,
there was no greater fate than to be a footnote
in the immense encyclopedia of barbarism,
that remains unappeased by barges rocking
on a famous embankment to the silent screeching
of concrete gargoyles and the dumb panic of flowers.
Parks named for kings. Gates closed against envy.

White walls set back amidst a mutter of birches
the house kept its cold secret—it had been
a cultural outpost in the old regime,
when the East was a colony of Russia.
But there was no partition in the sunshine
of the small rusty garden that a crow
crossed with no permit; instead, the folded echo
of interrogation, of conspiracy,
surrounded it, although its open windows
were steamed envelopes. This was another empire,
though a cold, not a hot one, and its relic
still gave me a November shudder. The shadow
of a cane-factory wheel shed by the pines
grew on the rough lawn. I sat on a plank bench
by the wooden table and listened to the sound
of papers being shuffled by an inquiry
into the parasitism of poetry by the dry-lipped leaves.
Then through the thinned trees I saw a wraith
of smoke, which I believed came from the house,
but every smoker carries his own wreath;
then I saw that this moving wreath was yours.
Another empire was finished. This time, Russia's.
Between the sighs of leaves shone the bones of birches.
I imagined your phantom in the alders, listening,
or, as the green phrase went: *unter den Linden.*
For History here is the covering-over of corpses,
not only in trenches of quicklime, but also
the dandruff of pigeon-drops in the stone-wigs of statues
composing minuets in the open, scoring sparrow-notes

on the page of a cloud, the flecks of blossom
on enamelled meadows the pages of spring,
a fusillade of skylarks in the smoking sky
and the screams of lilies harvested into a vase,
a sky composed of bandages and cotton
and the needles of sick spires, it is the music
heard in cold March through the black bars of lindens
by a remembering Jew, it is not only the cloud
but what is hidden under the cloud, under the page,
like the sinuous shadows of a sunken barge
in a sparkling canal, to the sound of a shovel
scraping over and tapping a small mound of error
which white flowers sprinkle to the sound of leaves
turning over and over in libraries in a new spring.

Breakfast 9:00 a.m. The whole terrace cool from the sea.
"And you go back to the States tomorrow?" "No. Milan."
"Not much to see in Milan," the waiter said.

III

"So, how was Italy?" My neighbor grinned.
Trim-bearded, elegant. He was Italian.
"Good. As usual. We were in Amalfi.
Next to a picturesque port called Vertigo."
He didn't get it. "Why didn't you stay longer?"
I said: "I have an island." "And it was calling you."
To say yes was stupidness, but it was true.
From the apartment I could see the Hudson.
Wide with its silent traffic, the silent buildings.

IV

Blue-grey morning, sunlight shaping Jersey,
and, magisterial, a white city gliding between buildings,
leaving the river for the Caribbean
its cargo: my longing. A high, immaculate ship.

PART II

7

I

Spiked palms rattle midsummer's consonants and
prose saunters down bougainvillea sidewalks,
and in a Spanish café, phrases at breakfast
translate the Village into Barranquilla.
We were assembled in the lobby of the hotel.
Constanzia nodded to her sergeant, who,
by a miracle of dentistry, had a dazzling grin
as brief as summer lightning in the mountains.
Her well-oiled hair was parted in the middle
as straight as the highway into Cartagena,
its black wings folded like a blackbird resting
on the telegraph wires, her large black eyes
were warm but cavernous; there were secrets in them,
the first was why she had become a soldier,
was she a mother or as I imagined
a young widow whose service was revenge?
There was a plump and rounded body
in that olive-green uniform. She took it off,
and, her hair loosened, took me to her cool breasts.
There was a quiet consternation among the palms
of Barranquilla. The plainclothes men were ready.
Cap on, she mounted and turned on her bike,
we got into the car with the plainclothes men

with the Ambassador and his assistant
and with Constanzia leading on her bike began
the careful, carfull exodus from Barranquilla.

II

The rebels were holed up in what was that city,
where the drug-lords had their shadow government
and the war was fiercest? No, not Alicante.
Something like it. Medellín. The infinite highway went
along the dry coast. The hours reeled back
along the road under the hot blue sky.
There were roadblocks set up against attack,
still picturesque despite the infantry.
As we shot along the mythological coast
the length of a line or a vine sprouted butterflies
the closer we got to aureate Cartagena.

On the long, desolate road before Cartagena,
desolate because of the drought, the khaki grass,
thorn scrub and dusty bush, and dull olive trees,
with an army patrol in camouflage uniforms
the colour of the country, very young Colombians,
by a highway cantina, the hillocks parched and dry
as a donkey's hide, some signs promising the sea,
burros loaded with grass trotting with concentration,
then another clot of soldiers, not quite a roadblock
signalling us on, then more and more arid pastures
with occasional zebu, light-skinned, with their humps,

the land dry and sour, where did they get their water?
Light traffic on the wind-whipped highway
from Barranquilla, all strange, all threatening,
and then a bright gap, an outburst and there it was
the white combers running and beaches through the trees—
the Caribbean, owned and exultant grinning and comforting
between sea-grape and sea-almonds and spindly palms
unguarded by soldiers. Not a new coast, but home.

III

It was pleasant in the car, even with the soldiers,
with the ladies gossipping; I wondered if they'd stop
to listen to the chatter of machine-gun fire
in case we were ambushed. Our bodyguards
scouted the patrol gulches and the scrub trees
although the patrol waved us through the roadblock
on the highway that shot into Cartagena. Earlier,
I had said goodbye to the beautiful plump soldier
whose hair, when she removed her forage cap,
was neatly parted as a blackbird's wings,
to the berry-red lipstick, goodbye to eyes
that held, I hoped, more than formal affection,
outside the hotel. Desire flashed from my face
like a weapon caught in sunlight, then she mounted
her lucky motorcycle and glided off, gone
into the turning traffic out of our lives.
Then we headed for the Caribbean coast.
African wind rattled the tin-coloured sea

to grooves of whitecaps, pounding the beach
closer to home—orange-walled Cartagena
or so I remember it. Our sea's first city.

IV

The afternoon raced with its shadows
across the *playa* and across the pitted face
of the old cathedral and the sidewalks
where vendors fanned themselves under the arches
all selling identical wares without rancour
or envy. Outside the piratical sea
blazed in tinfoil, and the shadows stopped
and settled in an eternity of langour.
Caravels slid over the horizon.
The flags of the sea-almonds wilted
and yard-smoke drifted, forked as Drake's beard,
sacker of Nombre de Dios.
Time, like a turtle, lay patient in the cool rocks.
The wing-beats of the great frigate were languid.
The covered cauldron of the sea hid—
ribbed galleons and turtles. Then later, our white skulls.

8

I

I saw the walled city early in the morning
with its sprinkled streets; under the arcades
the beggars slept, unshifting as History.
There was the city, then there was the magical
echo of the city's name and the same sulphurous
mirage of its double created by history,
by the shade of the rusting almonds, by the galvanized sea
whose ruts were left by the galleons, Cartagena
and the ghost of Cartagena; you could feel it shift
in the shadow of the almond on the open terrace,
in the sweet stink of the shallows by the sea-wall,
in the rough dark sand of the beach, the frowsty umbrellas
that echo a beach on the other side of the world,
drizzling Pescara, the light became a veil
through which phantoms moved, pirates and beggars
behind the high walls that hid Márquez's house.

II

Under a sea-almond's motley by the stone fort
with its embouchures for futile, rusted cannons,
the clouded water muttered its report

of piratical Cartagena, of New World Spain;
and, in the almond's restless shade, I thought
of Esperanza, would I see her again,
the small tight body and the astonished eyes,
as racing sunlight dried the stones of Venice,
Roberta; women who contained their cities.
What callipers fixed the terrestrial paradise?
I walked past them, past the fruit stands,
a vacillating compass. The old world
felt more familiar. Shame at heredity.
Drake. Nombre de Dios. A schoolboy's text.
The dusk struck gold and reminted the old fables.
But this one was shot in Medellín
and this one's daughter, a beauty,
was kept captive for a year and a half, for ransom
for which her family were still paying,
and then, what was nearer home,
on that golden road to the legendary city,
slums, shacks, a clogged river, El Dorados of garbage,
dirt tracks and canoes, the portals to paradise
to the walled city that was our Rome.
Unguarded by soldiers. Not a strange coast, but home.
The spikes of the agave: fear. A fear of flags.
And what if there is the body crumpled as usual
by the congealing gutter with the bloodstain
whose edges acquire the accuracy of a map,
and tires are still burning at the bend of an avenue
near to the haemophilic bougainvillea.

III

A shot rang out and the green Vespa skidded
off the curb into a ditch below a fence
of rusty cactus and the beautiful soldier lay
on the dry grass verge staring at the blue sky
with its puffs of cloud like echoes of an ambush
her forage cap off, and the quiet blackbird's wings
and the pomme-arac red lips appeared to make
a further beauty and a different peace.

That was the peace she carried in her eyes
that I mistook and hoped for, that was the look
whose calm contained a farewell, Constanzia,
a handshake magnified into this madness
that was the long brown street and the scabrous palms,
that was your country's discipline of sadness,
your coal-eyes dimming as you lay in my arms.

Her corpse had acquired that posture
in mimicry of your admirable syntax,
huddled in embarrassment at your contempt,
because it and the flies who were taking notes
and the mongrel conducting its private investigation
are all conscious of your prose, your style
that has the same self-conscious arches
of municipal buildings. Carrion and cactus
and the shivered palms at the folk-museum's entrance
and the smudged faces of the barefoot children,
their charred eyes smouldering like a pile of tires.

9

I

I lay on the bed near the balcony in Guadalajara
and watched the afternoon wind stiffen the leaves.
Later: dusty fields under parched lilac mountains
and clumps of what must have been eucalyptus
by the peeling skin of their barks. I saw your face,
I saw your flesh in theirs, my suffering brother;
jacaranda over the streets, all looking broken,
as if all Mexico had this film of dust,
and between trees dotting the plain, fog,
thick as your clogged breath, shrouding the ranges
of, possibly, Santa de Something. I read this.
March 11. 8:35 a.m. Guadalajara, Saturday.
Roddy. Toronto. Cremated today.
The streets and trees of Mexico covered with ash.
Your soul, my twin, keeps fluttering in my head,
a hummingbird, bewildered by the rafters,
barred by a pane that shows a lucent heaven.
The maid sings behind the house,
with wooden clips in her teeth,
she rips down laundry like an avenging angel
and the hillside surges, sailing. Roddy.
Where are you this bright afternoon? I
am watching a soccer match listlessly

on TV, as you did sunk deep in the socket of the sofa,
your head shrunken, your eyes wet
and every exchange an ordeal.

II

I carry a small white city in my head,
one with its avenues of withered flowers,
with no sound of traffic but the surf,
no lights at dusk on the short street
where my brother and our mother live now
at the one address, so many are their neighbours!
Make room for the accommodation of the dead,
their mounds that multiply by the furrowing sea,
not in the torch-lit catacombs of your head
but by the almond-bright, spume-blown cemetery.
What was our war, veteran of threescore years and ten?
To save the salt light of the island
to protect and exalt its small people
to sit enthroned to a clicking scissors
watching the hot road and the blue flowers across it
and behind the hedge soft blue mountains
and the barber with the face of a boxer
say one who loves his craft more than a victory
not like that arrogantly tilted tailor of Moroni's
assessing you with the eyes of his scissors.

III

The day, with all its pain ahead, is yours.
The ceaseless creasing of the morning sea,
the fluttering gamboge cedar leaves allegro,
the rods of the yawing branches trolling the breeze,
the rusted meadows, the wind-whitened grass,
the coos of the stone-coloured ground doves on the road,
the echo of benediction on a house—
its rooms of pain, its verandah of remorse
when joy lanced through its open-hearted doors
like a hummingbird out to the garden and the pool
in which the sky has fallen. These are all yours,
and pain has made them brighter as absence does
after a death, as the light heals the grass.
And the twig-brown lizard scuttles up its branch
like fingers on the struts of a guitar.
I hear the detonations of agave,
the stuttering outbursts of bougainvillea,
I see the acacia's bonfire, the begonia's bayonets,
and the tamarind's thorns and the broadsides of clouds from the
    calabash
and the cedars fluttering their white flags of surrender
and the flame trees' siege of the fort.
I saw black bulls, horns lowered, galloping, goring the mist
that rose, unshrouding the hillocks of Santa Cruz
and the olives of Esperanza,
Andalusian idyll, and answer
and the moon's blank tambourine
and the drizzle's guitars
and the sunlit wires of the rain

the shawls and the used stars
and the ruined fountains.

IV

When we were boys coming home from the beach,
it used to be such a thing! The body would be singing
with salt, the sunlight hummed through the skin
and a fierce thirst made iced water
a gasping benediction, and in the plated heat,
stones scorched the soles, and the cored dove hid
in the heat-limp leaves, and we left the sand
to its mutterings, and the long, cool canoes.

Threescore and ten plus one past our allotment,
in the morning mirror, the disassembled man.
And all the pieces that go to make me up—
the detached front tooth from a lower denture
the thick fog I cannot pierce without my glasses
the shot of pain from a kidney
these piercings of acute mortality.
And your wife, day and night,
assembling your accoutrements
to endure another day on the sofa,
bathrobe, glasses, teeth, because
your hands were leaves in a gust
when the leaves are huge-veined, desiccated,
incapable of protest or applause.
To cedars, to the sea that cannot change its tune,
on rain-washed morning what shall I say then

to the panes reflecting the wet trees and clouds
as if they were storefronts and offices, and
in what voice, since I now hear changing voices?
The change of light on a pink plaster wall
is the change of a culture—how the light is seen,
how it is steady and seasonless in these islands
as opposed to the doomed and mortal sun of midsummer
or in the tightening circle of shadow in the bullring.
This is how a people look at death
and write a literature of gliding transience
as the sun loses its sight, singing of islands.

Sunrise then, the uncontaminated cobalt
of sky and sea. The hours idle, and I,
watching the heaving plumes of the palmistes
in the afternoon wind, I hear the dead sighing
that they are still too cold in the ochre earth
in the sun's sadness, to the caterpillar's accordion
and the ancient courtship of the turtle-doves.
Yellow-billed egret balanced on a black bull
its sheen so ebony rust shines through the coat
as the bamboos translate the threshing of the olives
as the olives the bamboo's calligraphy
a silvery twitter of a flock of fledglings
stuttering for rain, wires of a drizzle,
tinfoil of the afternoon sea and the dove's bassoon.
The house on the hill opposite—
blond beams criss-cross their shadows on grey stone,
finical, full of false confidence, then
a surge of happiness, inexplicable content,
like the light on a golden garden outside Florence,

afternoon wind resilvering the olives
and the sea's doves, white sails
and the fresh elation of dolphins
over the staghorn coral.
Cartagena, Guadalajara,
whose streets, if one eavesdropped,
would speak their demotic Castilian
if dust had not powdered the eucalyptus with silences
on the iron balcony's parenthesis
and the Aztec mask of Mercedes
on the tip of the tongue like a sparrow
dipping into the pool
and flicking its tail like a signature, a name
like the fluttering of wings in a birdbath—
Santiago de Compostela!

V

In a swift receding year, one summer in Spain,
when the lamb-ribs were exquisitely roasted on a pine-fire
your eyes were its coals, your tongue its leaping flame,
my Iberian sibyl, touch-timid Esperanza.
A river roared from its dam, the pines were sprinkled
with its spume that brought boys' cries on the wind
drifting to our picnic and beyond the bank
was the brown spire of the cathedral
as a rose went out in the ashes
and the sunshine cooled and the wind had an edge
when a roar in the pines and the dam would blend
on the Saturday in Spain, in what receding year?

PART III

10

I

The ground dove stuttered for a few steps then flew
up from his path to settle in the sun-browned
branches that were now barely twigs; in drought it coos
with its relentless valve, a tiring sound,
not like the sweet exchanges of turtles in the Song
of Solomon, or the flutes of Venus in frescoes
though all the mounds in the dove-calling drought
the hills and gulches all briary and ochre
and the small dervishes that swivelled in the dust
were like an umber study for a fresco
of The Prodigal Son, this scorched, barren acre.
He had the smell of cities in his clothes,
the steam and soot of trains of Fascist stations
and their resounding vaults, he had the memory of rain
carried in his head, the rain on Pescara's beach
with the pastel hotels, and instead of the doves
the air-show with the jets soaring and swooping
over the Fair, the smell off that beach
came back on the rock-road where the turtle lifted
its mating music into the dry acacias,
and mixed with the smell off the galloping sea-flock,
each odour distinct, of sheep trampling their pens
as if their fear had caught the wolf-scent.

The rock-brown dove had fluttered from that fear
that what he loved and knew once as a boy
would panic and forget him from the change
of character that the grunting swine could smell.
A sow and her litter. Acknowledged prodigal.

Grey sunrise through a sky of frosted glass,
the great trees sodden, the paths below them pooled,
the headlands veiled and muslin-thin, no birds,
and pale green combers cresting through the drizzle;
a change of climate, the clouding of the self
in a sudden culture but one more confident
in its glazed equestrian statues in wet parks,
its railway stations echoing like the combers
in the ground-shaken caves under the cliff;
gathering, cresting then dissolving shallows
as light steps quietly into the house.
Light that inaudibly fits in the house
as a book on a bookshelf with its spines of tombs
and names, mouths slightly parted, eager to speak
wherever their station now. Every library
is a cemetery in sunlight. Sometimes, a shaft . . .

Across the dry hillock, leaves chasing dead leaves
in resurrecting gusts, or in the ochre quiet
leaves too many to rake on the road's margins,
too loaded to lift themselves, they lapsed singly
or in a yellow chute from the cedar, burnt branches;
lyres of desiccation choked the dry gutters
everywhere in the country, La Feuillée, Monchy,
by the caked track to Saltibus, over D'ennery.

Drought. Song of the wireless harp of the frangipani
that still makes a tangled music out of silence.

II

Now to cherish the depredations of April
even on the threshold of March, its sunlit eve—
the *gommier maudit* unshouldering its leaves,
barrow after loaded barrow, the leaves fading, yellow,
burnt grass and the tigerish shadows on the hillside,
and the azure a trowelled blue, and blue hill-smoke,
parched shortcuts and rust, cattle anchored in shadows
and groaning like winches, the didactic drought
against the hot sea that teaches what? Thirst
for the grace that springs in grooves of oblivious dust.

A fine haze screens the headland, the drizzle drifts.
Is every noun: breakwater, headland, haze,
seen through a gauze of English, a bright scrim,
a mesh in which light now defines the wires
and not its natural language? Were your life and work
simply a good translation? Would headland,
haze and the spray-wracked breakwater
pronounce their own names differently?
And have I looked at life, in other words,
through some inoperable cataract?
"What language do you speak in your own country?"
Every noun has its echo, a noun is a noise,
as every stone in the expanding sunlight
finds an exact translation in its shadow,

and it may be that you were halved by language
as definitively as the meridian
of Greenwich or by Pope Alexander's line,
but what makes this, if this is all it is,
more than just bearable, in fact, exultation
is the stone that is looked at, and the manchineels,
bitter, poisonous yellow berries, treacherous apples
that look like Eden's on the tree of knowledge
when the first noun was picked and named and eaten
and the shadow of knowledge defined every edge
originating language and then difference,
and subtlety, the snake and contradiction
and the sudden Babel of the manchineel.

III

The blank page grows a visionary wood.
A parallel section, no, in fact a whole province
of far, of foreign, of self-translating leaves
stands on the place where it has always stood
the right-hand margin of the page
loud, soft but voluble in their original language,
an orchestrating lexicon, veined manuscripts
going far back in time and deep in roots
and echoing in the tunnel of the right ear
with echoes: oak-echo, beech-echo, linden-echo,
and beech and birds a half-ancestral forest
whose metre was an ocean's and whose break,
parting declared the white-lined conjugation
of combers' centuries. This ocean, English and this forest weald,

this clattering natterer "burn," this distance, mist,
kept its high columns marching as my pen moves
towards that gap of light that comes upon
the bright salt arc of a bare unprinted beach
or where the piper leaves a print, its claws,
dim, imperceptible as an ancient rune—
that is the landscape, that, the stand of forest
made up of all these leaves and lines that
still rasp with delight with rhyme and incantation
pages of shade turning into translation.
And my left hand another vegetation
but not their opposite or their enemy,
palms and wild fern and praising them, the sea,
sea-almond, grape and vine and agave
that the wind's finger folded carefully
drawing its thumb to mark the dog-eared wave
across the dry hill, leaves chasing leaves
in a shiny, scurrying wind, and, in the brown quiet,
leaves, unraked, tiling the road's margins,
so loaded they don't lift, they lapse singly, yellow,
or chute from the cedars. Lyres of desiccation
in March's autumn, filling the dry gutters,
everywhere in the country, La Feuillée, Monchy,
except for the wireless harp of the frangipani
that still makes its music out of extreme stillness.
In my own botanic origins, *frangere panem*
to break bread, flower-flour in its white lilies,
except that in rare blossom I now remember
the flower is pink. It doesn't matter.
Since whatever hue it is, its wafer it serves that need,
petal on the sky's open palate at early mass

every morning but here most on this Sunday
with its Lenten drought, the heart-coloured flowers then
the caterpillars determinedly devour,
on a Sunday when a sadness still eats at the parallel
petals of my beaten heart, and the white pews of the sea,
the waves coming in aisles, my longing
for the communion of breakfast, the leafless,
flower-less but crusted bark of the frangipani,
frangere panem, the pain that I break and eat
flower and flour, pain and *pain*,
bright Easter coming, like the sea's white communion.

IV

In the country of the ochre afternoon
it is always still and hot, the dry leaves stirring
infrequently sometimes with the rattling pods
of what they call "women's tongues," in
the afternoon country the far hills are very quiet
and heat-hazed, but mostly in the middle
of the country of the afternoon I see the brown heat
of the skin of my first love, so still, so perfect,
so unaltered, and I see how she walked
with her sunburnt hands against the still sea-almonds,
to a remembered cove, where she stood on the small dock—
that was when I thought we were immortal
and that love would be folded doves and folded oars
and water lapping against eroding stone
in the ochre country of the afternoon.

11

I

The dialect of the scrub in the dry season
withers the flow of English. Things burn for days
without translation, with the heat
of the scorched pastures and their skeletal cows.
Every noun is a stump with its roots showing,
and the creole language rushes like weeds
until the entire island is overrun,
then the rain begins to come in paragraphs
and hazes this page, hazes the grey of islets,
the grey of eyes, the rainstorm's wild-haired beauty.

The first daybreak of rain, the crusted drought
broken in half like bread, the quiet trumpet mouth
of a rainbow and the wiry drizzle fighting
decease, half the year blowing out to sea
in hale, refreshing gusts, the withered lilies
drink with grateful mouths, and the first blackbird
of the new season announces itself on a bough
the hummingbird is reglistened drilling
the pierced hedges, my small shaft to your heart,
my emerald arrow: A crowd crosses a bridge
from Canaries to the Ponte Vecchio, from
Piaille to Pescara, and a volley of blackbirds

fans over Venice or the broken pier of Choiseul,
and love is as wide as the span of my open palm
for frontiers that read like one country,
one map of affection that closes around my pen.
I had forgotten the benediction of rain
edged with sunlight, the prayers of dripping leaves
and the cat testing the edge of the season
with careful paw. And I have nothing more
to write about than gratitude. For *la mer*,
soleil-là, the bow of the *arc-en-ciel*
and the archery of blackbirds from its
radiant bow. The rest of the year is rain.

II

"There was a beautiful rain this morning."
"I was asleep."
                    He stroked her forehead.
She smiled at him, then laughed as she kept yawning.
"It was lovely rain." But I thought of the dead
I know. The sun shone through the rain
and it was lovely.
                    "I'm sure," she said.
There were so many names the rain recited:
Alan, Joseph and Claude and Charles and Roddy.
The sunlight came through the rain and the drizzle shone
as it had done before for everybody.
For John and Inge, Devindra and Hamilton.
"Blessed are the dead that the rain rains upon,"
wrote Edward Thomas. Her eyes closed in my arms,

but it was sleep. She was asleep again,
while the bright rain moved from Massade to Monchy.

Sometimes I stretch out, or you stretch out your hand,
and we lock palms; our criss-crossed histories join
and two maps fit. Bays, boundaries, rivers, roads,
one country, one warm island. Is that noise rain
on the hot roof, is it sweeping out to sea
by the stones and shells of the almond cemetery?

III

The road is wet, the leaves wet, but the sun inching,
and always the astonishment: in March?
This blustery, this grey? The waves chopping
and circling and ramming into one another
like sheep in a maddened pen from a whiff of wolf,
or white mares, bug-eyed from the lightning's whip,
and, if they could, whinnying. But the light will win.
The sun fought with the rain in the leaves and won;
then the rain came back and it was finer out to sea.
A drizzle blurred the promontories evenly
and now the manchineels and acacias sparkled
with the new rain and the cows' hides darkened
as the horses dipped their heads and shook their manes,
and over the horizon the faint arc
of an almost imperceptible bow appeared
then dimmed across the channel towards Martinique.
This miracle was usual for the season.
"The sun came out just for you," he said.

And it was true. The light entered her forehead
and blazoned her difference there.
The pastures were beaded, roofs shone on the hills,
a sloop was working its way against huge clouds
as patches of sunlight widened with a new zeal
towards detachment, towards simplicity.
Who said that they were lying side by side,
the cupped spoon of her torso in his own
in the striped shadows of mid-afternoon?

IV

The doors are open, the house breathes and I feel
a balm so heavy and a benediction
so weightless that the past is just blue air
and cobalt motion lanced with emerald
and sail-flecks and the dove's continuous complaint
about repletion, its swollen note of gratitude—
all incantation is the monody of thanks
to the sky's motionless or moving altars,
even to the faint drone of that silver insect
that is the morning plane over Martinique,
while, take this for what you will, the frangipani
that, for dry months, contorted, crucified
in impotence or barrenness, endured, has come
with pale pink petals and blades of olive leaves,
parable of my loin-longing, my silver age.

From the salt brightness of my balcony
I look across to the abandoned fort;

no History left, just natural history,
as a cloud's shadow subtilizes thought.
On a sloped meadow lifted by the light,
the Hessians spun like blossoms from the immortelle,
the tattered pennons of the sea-almond fluttered
to the spray-white detonations of the lilac
against blue the hue of a grenadier, dried pods
of the flamboyant rattle their sabres
and a mare's whinny across the parched pastures
launches white scuds of sails across the channel,
the race of a schooner launched in a canal.
A grey sky trawls its silver wires of rain;
these are the subtleties of the noon sea:
lime, emerald, lilac, cobalt, ultramarine.

12

I

Prodigal, what were your wanderings about?
The smoke of homecoming, the smoke of departure.
The earth grew music and the tubers sprouted
to Sesenne's singing, rain-water, fresh patois
in a clay carafe, a clear spring in the ferns,
and pure things took root like the sweet-potato vine.
Over the sea at dusk, an arrowing curlew,
as the sun turns into a cipher from a green flash,
clouds crumble like cities, the embers of Carthage;
any man without a history stands in nettles
and no butterflies console him, like surrendering flags,
does he, still a child, long for battles and castles
from the books of his beginning, in a hieratic language
he will never inherit, but one in which he writes
"Over the sea at dusk, an arrowing curlew,"
his whole life a language awaiting translation?

Since I am what I am, how was I made?
To ascribe complexion to the intellect
is not an insult, since it takes its plaid
like the invaluable lizard from its background,
and if our work is piebald mimicry
then virtue lies in its variety

to be adept. On the warm stones of Florence
I subtly alter to a Florentine
till the sun passes, in London
I am pieced by fog, and shaken from reflection
in Venice, a printed page in the sun
on which a cabbage-white unfolds, a bookmark.
To break through veils like spiders' webs,
crack carapaces like a day-moth and achieve
a clarified frenzy and feel the blood settle
like a brown afternoon stream in River Doree
is what I pulsed for in my brain and wrist
for the drifting benediction of a drizzle
drying on this page like asphalt, for peace that passes
like a changing cloud, to a hawk's slow pivot.

II

In the vale of Santa Cruz I look to the hills.
The white flowers have the fury of battle,
they lay siege to the mountains, for war
there is the tumult of the white ravines,
and the cascade's assault; they bow their plumes,
Queen Anne's lace, bougainvillea, orchid and oleander,
and they are as white as arrested avalanches,
angry and Alpine, their petals blur into
a white gust from the Matterhorn or the streets of Zermatt.
Both worlds are welded, they were seamed by delight.
Santa Cruz, in spring. Deep hills with blue clefts.
I have come back for the white egrets
feeding in a flock on the lawn, darting their bills

in that finical stride, gawkily elegant,
then suddenly but leisurely sailing
to settle, but not too far off, like angels.

III

I wake at sunrise to angelic screams.
And time is measuring my grandchildren's cries
and time outpaces the sepia water
of the racing creek, time takes its leisure, cunning
in the blocked hollows of the pool, the elephantine stones
in the leaf-marked lagoon, time sails
with the soundless buzzard over the smoking hills
and the clouds that fray and change
and time waits very quiet between the mountains
and the brown tracks in the valleys of the Northern Range,
a cover of overhanging bamboo, in Maraval
where, if the bed were steeper, a brown stream races
or tries to, pooling in rocks, with great avail
for me at least, or where a range's blues
and indigo over which wide hawks sail
their shadows on the wells of Santa Cruz,
dark benedictions on the brook's muttering shale,
and the horses are slowly plunging their manes
as they climb up from the paved-with-lilies pond,
so much mythology in their unharnessed necks!
These little things take root as I add my praise
to the huge lawn at the back of the house, a field,
a bright, unaltered meadow, a small savannah
for cries and bicycles and joy-crazed dogs

bolting after pedalling boys, the crescent ghost
of the new moon showing and on the thick slopes
this forest like green billowing smoke
pierced by the flame petals of the immortelle.

IV

Petals of the flame tree against ice-cream walls
and the arches across the park with its tacit fountain,
the old idlers on the benches, this is the prose
that spreads like the shade of an immortal banyan
in front of the library, the bulk that darkens
the violin of twilight when traffic has vanished
and nearly over also the colonial regime when the wharves
cradled the rocking schooners of our boyhood to
the echo of vespers in the alien cathedral.
In the hot green silence a dragonfly's drone
crossing the scorched hill to the shade of the cedars
and spiced laurels, the *lauriers canelles*,
the word itself lifting the plurals of its leaves,
from the hot ground, from this page, the singeing smells.
How simple to write this after you have gone,
that your death that afternoon had the same ease
as stopping at the side of the road under the trees
to buy cassava bread that comes in two sorts,
sweet and unsweetened, from the huge cauldron,
on the road between Soufrière and Canaries.
The heat collects in the depths between the ridges
and the high hawks circle in the gathering haze;
like consonants round a vowel, insistent midges

hum round a noun's hexagon, and the hornet's house.
Delve in the hot, still valley of Soufrière,
the black, baking asphalt and its hedges dripping shade
and here is the ultimate nullity despite the moil
of the churning vegetation. The small church
hidden in leaves. In mid-afternoon, the halt—
then dart of a quizzical lizard across the road.

13

I

Flare of the flame tree and white egrets stalking.
Small bridge, brown trace, the new fire station.
And the clatter of parrots at sunrise
and at dusk their small wild souls returning
to the darkening trees, the pouis
against the Santa Cruz hills, orange and vermilion.
And great cities receding, Madrid, Genoa,
and their aisles with soaring arches
in the naves of shadow, the bamboo's basilica
the pillars of palmistes, Doric and Corinthian,
no, the point is not comparison or mimicry
in the incantations of fronds, nor the wafer-receiving
palms of the breadfruit, it is not in the envy
of hazed hills jealous of snow, not in the
pliant, surrendering lances of the cane
at Breda, not the indigo ignorance
that the ridges contain, because in what language
should the white herons talk, and with whose anger
do the wild parrots scream, who has tormented them
as mercilessly as we have tortured ourselves
with our conflicts of origins? Fill
the vessel of the egret with oblivious milk
and drink to the amnesia of Asia

with its yellow beaker, and listen, this time
to the correcting imprecations of the high palms:
"You are all mistaken, that is not what we are saying,
our prayers are not for you, there is nothing imperial
in our plumes, not for the horsemen of Bornu,
and the shells have no secret, and all your pages flutter
with the hysteria of parrots. Listen, we have
no envy of the white mountains, or of the white horn
above the smothered inns, no envy of the olive
or redoubtable oaks. We were never emblems.
The dawn would be fresh, the morning bliss,
if the light would break on your glaucous eyes
to see us without a simile, not just the green world
or streams where the pebbles are parables
and a plank bridge less than the Ponte Vecchio
or the motley of cocoa, its jester's hues and tatters
less than the harlequins in that *Rigoletto*
which elated you in Parma, or the slow haze of rain
that dried on the salty esplanade of Pescara,
or the darkness of Bosnia in the clouds of Santa Cruz.
The inheritance which you were sent to claim
defined itself in contradiction; there in that hall
among those porcelain-pink and dour burghers
was an illegitimate ancestor, as equal
as the African fishing through tall river-reeds
to pierce you, threshing on his stick."

II

And the first voice replied in the foam:
"What is culture if not the horizontal light
of magnificent gardens, statues dissolving in dusk
and fountains whose jets repeat an immortal phrase
to you, vague pilgrim? In long halls,
in incredible colonnades, the busts and portraits
will exist even if they were not looked at, perspectives
indifferent to your amazement. What is immortal
is what does not need your presence to assess it,
including these lines, even if you were never
disenchanted by the weather in Santiago de Compostela
or the mischievous drizzle on the dull esplanade
of banal Pescara, but you have caught an illness:
the malaria of dusk whose statues never shiver
or cough in the cold, or tremble with influential aspens,
and you will die from this indifference;
the horn of the white mountain above Zermatt
has gored you, and the lamps shine like blood drops
and the mantle rapidly climbs shrouding the snow
when memory blows out its candle
you can feel Europe drawn slowly over your cold brow."

III

So has it come to this, to have to choose?
The chafe of the breakers' moving marbles,
their lucent and commodious statuary
of turbulent stasis, changing repetition

of drizzling spray that glazes your eyes
like the marble miracles of the Villa Borghese?
Do not diminish in my memory
villages of absolutely no importance,
the rattling bridge over the stone-bright river,
un-ornate churches, chapels in the provinces
of light-exhausted Europe. Hoard, cherish
your negligible existence, your unrecorded history
of unambitious syntax, your clean pools
of unpolluted light over close stones.

IV

The sound of Paris in the rustling trees
when the leaves talk traffic and the withered pods
of the acacias are dried spices in the cafés
that season reputation; "You don't know Paris?"
"No. Never been there." "You've got to go."
"Why?"
        More repulsion: "Why?"
               "Yeah. Why?"
"Because it's Paris, that's why."
            "I see."
"No, you don't see, you're being stubborn."
"Maybe when I get there I'll see."
"It will change your life."
        "I like my life."
"You think here is enough?"
        "For me it is."

"Fine."

"Anyway I can see Martinique from here."

For approbation had made me an exile.
In some ways it was like a lamp going out,
or rather the bright leaf of a candle withering
from a bright vermilion to a thinning blue,
and then extinction, then the loss of joy,
but joy in what? In the island or in Italy?
In the impossibility of, implausibility of,
Roberta's Venice or Esperanza's Spain
or walks by some shade-striped leafy canal
with attendant barges. Never to have seen them
or seen her, the orange flame of their cities—
a wall alert in dusk with its candle-spires
blown into acceptable oblivion.
The huge doors close of the immense museum
the clock face of the bullring contracts its shadow
and yet it is the same sun that lets the cliffs
of Canaries plunge into a blue dusk, as day blows out,
and the lights of tiny dwellings riddle the Morne.
Cherish their foreheads, the brow's blank openness,
that you shared adoration. Yet what was adored,
the city or its women? Aren't they the same,
and without the candle in the heart still bending
like a moving altar towards the admired
in the love that has no epoch, no history?
No question. And are both places blent?
Blent into this, whatever this thing is?

And the cracked heart and the dividing mind
yawn like a chasm, from too many fissures
like the blanched Alps or in the khaki drought
a *falaise* in Choiseul, around D'elles Soeurs.

14

I

From a blue keg, the barrel's thumb-tuned goatskin,
the choirs of ancestral ululation
are psalms and pivot for the prodigal
in a dirt yard at Piaille, are confrontation,
old incantation and fresh sacrifice
where a ram is tethered, without the scrolled horns,
wool locks and beard of the scapegoat,
in the Old Testament, or black blood gushing in a trench
in Attic ceremony and rite. Death softens the eyes
of the still, unbleating sheep, a common ewe,
as for you this is common. There is no awe
in repetition, no claim, no tribal ecstasy,
no pardon in the bent smoke from Guinea,
the sprinkled white rum, or the meal crumbled
on the small stone altar, in the broken memory
of the slaver's coast and the braided villages
of thatch and coalpot from the salted passage
to this paralysis where your pale feet cannot keep time
feel no communion with its celebrants,
they keep another time, the time you keep
comes with a different metre, your skin
what sheath and prison that it has become

as a dried chrysalis with no resurrection
and one unwished for. Star-embers fade.

II

I could give facts and dates, but to what use?
In the lush chasms and fissures of Choiseul
an ogre bred my grandam, whelped my father,
erected my tall aunts; slopes with potato vines,
and the narrow, clean dark water of River Doree,
the fragrant hogplums and chapel of La Fargue;
go in search of his own shire, unlatch a gate
that opens into Albion, its faery flowers,
its source of intellectual bastardy,
without embarrassment or degradation,
without belligerence or accusation,
and mostly selfishly, without self-contempt,
a curious and self-nourishing integer
outside their given numbers and their dates,
as nameless as the bush, beyond heredity
or prophecy, or the quiet panic of clocks,
the shallow penitence of mirrors. Mongrel.
And out of this chord, this discord will come
the Atlantic's drone, the Caribbean hum
of chaos in an ochre afternoon
the enclosing harmony that we call home
when the sea mints its quicksilver, when
the cedars sag and the light ends up with nothing.
The facts! The Facts! The history. The cause.
You need a history to make your case.

III

1492. 1833. 1930.
Dates. The one thing about which there is no discourse.
Dates multiplied by events, by consequences,
are what add up to History. We have a few coins
struck for a mere handful of events,
as amateur numismatists, regal profiles,
none worthy in the traditional way of memory,
slavery being an infinity of endeavour
without pause or payment, without commemoration,
only the long division of day into dark,
of drought into rainburst, equinoxes glide
over their own shadows, and all our dates,
our calendars, hymns and anniversaries,
were bequeathed to us. Left to itself
the brain would be mantled like coral in the cool
shade of a reef's outcrop and turret, swayed
like reeds in meditation, dateless.
The petals of the sun curl, wilting on its stalk—
here comes the quiet lily crescent of the moon.

IV

From this thick tree issues miraculous bread.
The breadfruit makes itself from copious shade,
whose dial is the ground's dry, palmate leaves,
a voluble, invaluable dome, a library,
where all the town's talk is stored,
and in whose core is coiled—a tempest,

a rising sea in wind, the spinning pages
of remorseful texts, Bligh's log and cannonballs
and bowling thunder, shelter from the rain
and so magnanimous in circumference
that it has no time without shade, and shade
is suffering. The sun makes their suffering mute.
This bedraggled backyard, this unfulfilled lot,
this little field of leaves, brittle and fallen,
of all the cities of the world, this is your centre.
O to be luminous and exact! As this tree is
in ripening sunshine, that your own leaves could shine
with nourishment, and give such shade and peace,
the mirror of each canvas that you sign.
Despite acclamation, despite contempt,
I was never part of that catalogue
in spite of friends in the same business
neither of the free-verse orthodoxy, nor the other—
the clogged, elegiac thickness of memory;
farther away from all that, forever,
knee-high in the foam of the page
wading by sounding caves.
Gradually it hardens, the death-mask of Fame.

V

And Sancta Trinidad. It is that sacred to me.
However fragmentary, through a sunlit hedge,
by the running of clear water over the sun-wiry stones
and a cool hoarding of bamboos without a bridge
phrases of Spain in summer, in the vale of Santa Cruz,

perhaps because of the name, but the bamboo's fountains
arch, sounding sweet, surreptitious, twittering leaves
and shadows moving over indigo mountains.

In a green street of hedges and vermilion roofs,
and gates that creak open into banana yards
and doors that groan on the evocation of ginger
behind which are the hill with five cresting palms
whose long fingers are stirring tropical almanacs
darkened with rain over the grey savannahs
of zebu and bison and the small chalk temples
of an almost erased Asia, and the ovations of cane
through which turbaned horsemen carry feathering lances.
The cloud-white egret, the heron whose hue
is wet slate, move through a somnolence
as sweet as malaria to a child whose parched lips
are soothed by a servant or his own mother,
to the sudden great sound of rain on the roofs,
cloudburst of benediction, dry seas in his ears.

15

I

Ritorno a Milano, if that's correct.
Past the stalagmites of the Duomo
the peaches of summer are bouncing
on the grids of the Milanese sidewalks
in halters cut close to the coccyx.
I look and no longer sigh for the impossible,
panting over a cupidinous coffee
like an old setter that has stopped chasing pigeons
up from the piazza. The skirts fly from me
without actual levitation, the young waiter
scrapes the crumbs of my years from the tablecloth.

Old man coming through the glass, who are you?
I am you. Learn to acknowledge me,
the cottony white hair, the heron-shanks,
and, when you and your reflection bend,
the leaf-green eyes under the dented forehead,
do you think Time makes exceptions, do you think
Death mutters, "Maybe I'll skip this one"?
the same silent consequence that crept across
your brother perilously sleeping, and all the others
whose silence is no different from your brother's.

There is an old man standing in the door glass there,
silent beyond raging, beyond bafflement,
past faith, whose knees easily buckle,
toothless at sunrise with white knotted hair,
who sometimes feels his flesh cold as the stone
that he will lie under, there where the sea-almonds
blaze in drought, and where a radiant sea
in an inexplicable exultation
exclaims its joy, and where the high cemetery
of marble clouds moves ponderously, lightly,
as if that were a heaven for old men
where those who have left await him,
cities of clouds and ghosts and whatever they mean.
All of the questions tangle in one question.
Why does the dove moan or the horse shake its mane?
Or the lizard wait on the white wall then is gone?

II

In my effort to arrive at the third person
has lain the ordeal; because whoever the "he" is,
he can suffer, he can make his own spasms, he can die;
I can look at him and smile incontrollably.
I can study the blotches on his hands,
his multiplying moles, his netted eyes,
the gestures that observe the predictions of fiction
in resting a cup of coffee in its saucer,
e'n la sua volontade è nostra pace,
in His will is our pizza.

Grey barges under grey sky on the grey river.
And like the Irish beauty's signature,
a cirrus sky scrawled with longing for return.

III

Lemons of Montale against an ochre wall
in a garden raging with dragonflies.
This is your city of annual invitations
predictably in spring or the sweat-beads of summer
when skins are turning brown and sunglasses
repeat anonymity, and that avenue of elms
or broad-shouldered oaks whose name you haven't learnt
moves from temperate to tropical, when awnings unfurl
with an exultant rattle and umbrellas open
like wooden sunflowers near the beehive of the Duomo
in Mediterranean Milan pretending it is Nice;
so an adopted city slides into me,
till my gestures echo those of its citizens,
and my shoes that glide over a sidewalk grating
move without fear of falling, move as if rooted
in the metre of memory, of Milanese motion,
without longing for Florence, walking on the water
of a Venice crammed with churches, walking
in the agitation of the ordinary,
in the excitement of boredom. Not only cupolas
define a great city, but also lanes
where we think we are lost, guided by Paola,
of brown and ochre cul-de-sacs, no no this is not
the restaurant this is some kind of Academy

away from the traffic, with, say, a bright tree
alert in sunshine, let's call it a linden,
or a chestnut or plane-tree, then, most alarming:
something close to a palmiste in its heraldry
its Corinthian coils, a palm like an amen
to which I still can never say home,
as generous as it is, as close, that has become,
across a furled map, the compass of my heart.

IV

Verona, Bremerio, Campogalliano,
my mind goes down that side-road in the sun.
Who struggled there, in that decayed farmhouse
with eyeless windows and a tongueless door
that once spoke Latin, its roof crusted with rust
and crumbled walls the colour of dead straw,
road where their sandals raised a fading dust?
Who marched there, what lances, what standards
filed through the rattling maize where the mole hid,
the vole scuttered or the brown hawk
soared with a rusted scream and the velvet otter
left O O O o.

At breakfast on the white terrace in Rimini
the young waitress was a replica of my first love—
the jutting lower lip, its provocative pout,
the streaks of blond hair, the Asiatic cheekbones,
and slanted sea-grey eyes the Adriatic.
Christ, over fifty years. Half of a century!

It was forever morning on the harbour
and there was only one subject—Time.
Then Italy was the gamboge cubes of brick
that were the old cantonment, a corner of Giorgione,
above the clear dance of Botticelli waves.

16

I

Sunlight on the buildings on the hills over Genoa
in the chill spring, the gulls know each other.
Where the open channel breaks into high spray
and a sailor dips deeper and higher on the bowsprit
clouds will congeal into islands, the rattling anchor-chain
of an archipelago; Genoa thins.
As Genoa thins, everything diminishes,
the mountains, the dry hill with its castle.

In those small, missal-sized booklets
mostly in ochre monochrome, stone-pocked
and bristling hillocks showed a landscape
tufted with cypresses and dusty poplars
and roads with tiny cantering horsemen
and cuts with tiny horsemen cantering
towards a castle, and overhead and emblems
in the cracked blue, a bird flock halted,
as wind spins their pages backwards into spray.

II

A grey dawn, dun. Rain-gauze shrouding the headlands.
A rainbow like a bruise through cottony cumuli.
Then, health! Salvation! Sails blaze in the sun.
A twin-sailed shallop rounding Pigeon Island.
This line is my horizon.
I cannot be happier than this.

III

There is this fine, invisible drizzle on the sea
almost hazing the headland and he feels
that humming that goes on in the tired heart
once you are home; between distance and time
it had to come; so, as for my Venetian,
it is farewell to her, if not to Canaletto,
to the silvery-green wavelets of the busy lagoon
hecting with poling gondolas, farewell black hair
with its glints of rust, to sighing bridges,
to the fresco's sky, as cracked as his heart.

IV

I have been blent in the surface of the frescos,
in the cracked halos, the tight, eternal gestures—
admonishing finger, creaseless brow, in the folds
of a sea-blue mantle, in hilltop turrets
and a resting fly. So, when I am dissolved,

what is that dissolution? My race, my sun?
The precipices of my island, that, despite themselves,
mimic the fissures of Reggio Calabria,
to feel my skin change, my delight translated?
Museums are the refuge of the prodigal.
I am not made subtly Italian, there is no betrayal,
there is no contradiction in this surrender,
nor heredity in delight in the knuckles of a Mantegna
or abounding Botticellian locks, nor that housefly
in the corner of Crivelli; O prodigal,
your momentary statue made by a traffic light
on that sunlit corner across from the newspaper kiosk
where the glass bank prints your transient reflection,
less permanent than a frame from Ghirlandaio!

17

I

Into this fishing village, the hot zinc of noon,
its rags of shadow, the reek from its drains,
and the mass of flies around the fish-market,
where ribbed dogs skitter sideways,
is this one where you vowed a life-long fealty,
to the bloated women with ponderous breasts
and the rum-raddled, occasional fishermen,
over an ochre alley near the walls of Parma,
with the monumental portrait of Giuseppe Verdi?
What did you swear to uphold? This filth?
Or the aria that soars like a banner from its gates?

There was a vow I made, rigid apprentice,
to the horizontal sunrise, acolyte
to the shallows' imprecations, to the odour
of earth turned by the rain, to the censer of mist,
to the pennons of cocoa, though I hated its darkness,
to the wrist of a cold spring between black rocks,
and any road that lost its mind in the mountains,
to the freight train of the millipede, to
the dragonfly's biplane, and the eel's submarine,
as the natural powers I knew, swearing not to leave them
for real principalities in Berlin or Milan,

but my craft's irony was in betrayal,
it widened reputation and shrank the archipelago
to stepping stones, oceans to puddles, it made
that vow provincial and predictable
in the light of a silver drizzle, in, say, Pescara.

II

Compare Milan, compare a glimpse of the Arno,
with this river-bed congealed with rubbish.
I have seen Venice trembling in the sun,
shadow-shawled Granada and the cork groves of Spain,
across the coined Thames, the grey light of London,
the drizzles sweeping Pescara's esplanade
and stone dolphins circling the basin of a fountain,
but, on the sloping pastures behind Gros Piton,
in the monumental shadow of that lilac mountain,
I have seen the terrestrial paradise.
And why waste all that envy when they take
as much pride in their suffering as in their cathedrals,
a vanity indifferent to proportions?
I have seen me shift from empire to empire;
I should have known that I would wind up beached
as I began on the blazing sand
rejected by the regurgitating billows
retreating with their long contemptuous hiss
for these chaotic sentences of seaweed
plucked by the sandpiper's darting concentration.
Be the one voice; the white Alps and the lace
of blossoms blown past the hotel window

or the leaves from the train window where you sat
through which you saw the ghost that is now your face
the poui's petals in the street lights of Zermatt.

O Altitudino! And my fear of heights.
But in Zermatt it was the clear, dry cold
that is the delight of skiers and of angels
over riven crevices where the old snow was packed
and the new snow almost blinded. Not different,
the one celestial, real geography.

III

The light itself looks tired on the water tower,
and all delight exhausted in the craft,
and from a life-long siege of the theatre
dull detonations of bewildering failure,
limpness and lassitude, the mockery of power,
paralysis of the unfinished draft.
But strength will fill your wrist again, be sure,
and one last effort pull the world around
with the helm locked and adversity, reversed,
cross its own wake into the wider quiet
of an emerald inlet where the only sound
is of your mast swaying in the creaking wind.
Dusk growing rose, afternoon's sliding eclipse
on the Hudson's crinkled excelsior, the bluffs of Jersey,
the dusk growing more Dutch over ditch and water,
an epoch absorbs me into its enamelled sky,
the light on the flanks of a herd, on the vanes of a mill.

From grey Geneva and its lake of stones
from its invisible but certain opposite shore
for being swallowed up in fog, in distance
already spectres, banal metaphor,
walking along its flag-flapping streets
a figure in white fog dividing this page
which again enclosed you, which again repeats
your figure waiting on the landing stage
fingering the obols in your pockets,
remorseless revenant, the orange water burning
from the garlanded bridges as the sun sets—
the small ferry with its empty seats returning.
In shrouded, spectral Stockholm, across the bridge,
with the lights coming on in the Opera House,
and on the ferries, the brisk folk in black,
lights of branches beaded with orange berries
the smoke puffing out from their faces
making them incurable addicts; from Milan
to spires needling us on the far horizon
we are distant. They soar as we approach,
and their height diminishes us. All corners soon
become familiar again, the river, the river's glittering reach.
The secular naves of bridges, and because it is fall,
or spring, or even the icicled branches
in their silence which are like waiting crystal
the city we both loved gives back the same answers
to the living, but as to who is dead,
ah, that is the riddle, the mute anguish, the enigma!
The stores glide past and the bird-watching head
of some anonymous statue endures the stigma
of a different silence. I still cannot subtract

a single dishevelled digit from the mass, from the sight
of you, with a cigarette and your raincoat and tonsure
obeying, like them, the changing of the light
crossing with me, so calmly, to the other shore.

IV

You never think of January as a stormy month,
but the African wind blows rain across the cape,
the combers come in fast and their high surf
explodes irregularly along the Causeway.
It is the season of rainbows, of a thin drizzle
in the wet air; so many, their backs arch
like radiant dolphins, they leap over the hills
above the villages, profuse with benediction,
over the hissing sea and the small fine roads
and the indigo ranges heavy with the darkening rain.
But now, even farther north, in Bimini
it would be clearer, finer, without a haze
over the lime-green shallows and the violet reefs
and the dark chasms full of wavering reeds,
and the abyss of my deep cowardice,
my fears and treacheries in an old age
foam-crested with conspiring murmurings
subliminal, submarine, when my ageing prayer
is, hooked to this craft, to break clear of the nets
to shudder like a great convulsive marlin
into heaven and fall crashing and leap again
scattering prisms and led by veering dolphins
vault for the last time breaking free of the line.

V

Be happy; you're writing from the privilege
of all your wits about you in your old age,
under the thorn acacias by the noon sea,
the light on all the places you have painted
and hope to paint with the strenuous accuracy
of joy, the village houses, the streets untainted
by any history, by any thought or shadow
on the blank canvas except from the sky;
be grateful that each craft stays hard to do.
In what will be your last book make each place
as if it had just been made, already old,
but new again from naming it: the gaping view
of the bay with its toy yachts at Marigot,
and the plunge into the rich banana valley
under the haze-blue ridges into Roseau,
or how, from tortuous curves after Choiseul,
the corners levelled into spacious country
wide with the wind that makes the combers swell
and wreathes the beach with kale around Vieuxfort.
My eyes are washed clean in the sea-wind, I feel
brightness and sweet alarm, the widened pupils
of the freshly familiar, things that have not moved
since childhood, nouns that have stayed
to keep me company in my old age.
What if our history is so rapidly enclosed
in bush, devoured by green, that there are no signals
left, since smoke, the smoke of encampments
by brigand and the plumes from muskets
are transitory memorials and our forests shut

their mouths, sworn to ancestral silence.
Its fugitives were nomadic, their callused soles
raked out their cooking fires, and what a great gulf
of loyalty of inheritance comes from that fact—
that these are your ancestors, not the cloaked pilgrims
of the one time in aureate Venice or the blest stones
of your Via Veneto, nor in sanctified ruins,
nor the grace of filigreed twilight on the Duomo,
nor the pompous claim staked out for the Pyramids!
Your only legendary deserts are those dunes
from which there dribbles a funnel of sand
as into an hour-glass that scares a crab,
but you felt in your calling that from your hand
the seeded word would overrun these ruins and
sprout with the fecundity of bougainvillea.

18

I

Grass, bleached to straw on the precipices of Les Cayes,
running in the blue and green wind of the Trade,
a small church hidden in a grove past Soufrière,
hot dasheen and purpling pomme arac,
and heavy cattle in a pasture, and the repetition
of patois prayers by the shallows of Troumassee,
and there are still her eyes waiting for the small lights
that bring them to life, in which are reflected
the gold glints of labels in the Folies-Bergère bar
and the rust and orange of an April Glory cedar,
the leaves falling like curses from the *gommier maudit*,
a gull plucking fish from the shallows,
in the distance, the hump of a hazed mountain,
the ochreing meadows and the continuous cresting
of combers coming in, leaves spinning in the breeze
and the spray steadily spuming, the jets of bougainvillea,
all these must mould her cheekbones and a mouth
that says, "I come from Mon Repos," from Saltibus,
from the curve of the road entering Canaries
and from the white nights of an insomniac Atlantic
that toss on the reefs of Praslin, that made me.
O blessed pivot that makes me a palm!
A silent exclamation at the cliff's edge

around whom the horizon silently spins!
What thuds against the hull, butting with such force?
Angels are gliding underneath the keel.

II

Time, that gnaws at bronze lions and dolphins
that shrivels fountains, had exhausted him;
a cupola in Milan exhaled him like incense,
Abruzzi devoured him, Firenze spat him out,
Rome chewed his arm and flung it over her shoulder
for the rats in the catacombs; Rome took his empty eyes
from the sockets of the Colosseum. Italy ate him.
Its bats at vespers navigated her columns
with an ancient elation, a hand in San Marco's font
aspersed him with foul canal water, then bells
tossed their heads like bulls, and their joy
rattled the campaniles, as innumerable pigeons
settled on the square of his forehead, his kidneys
were served in a modest hotel in Pescara,
a fish mimicked his skeleton in salty Amalfi,
until after a while there was nothing left of him
except this: a name cut on a wall that soon
from the grime of indifference became indecipherable.

III

We were headed steadily into the open sea.
Immeasurable and unplummetable fathoms

too deep for sounding or for any anchor,
the waves quick-running, crests, we were between
the pale blue phantoms of Martinique and Saint Vincent
on the iron rim of the ringing horizon;
the farther we went out, the white bow drumming,
plunging and shearing spray, the wider my fear,
the whiter my spume-shot cowardice, as the peaks
receded, rooted on their separating world,
diminishing in the idea of home, but still the prow
pressed stubbornly through the gulfs and the helmsman
kept nodding in their direction through the glass
between the front deck and the wheel, their direction
meaning what we could not see but he knew was there
from talking on the radio to the other boat
that lay ahead of us towards which we plunged
and droned, a white slip of another smaller cruiser,
convinced by his smiling that we would breach them soon.
"Dolphins," the steersman said. "You will see them playing,"
but this was widening into mania, there were only
the crests that looked to their leaping, no fins,
no arching backs, no sudden frieze, no school today,
but the young captain kept on smiling, I had never
seen such belief in legend, and then, a fin-hint!
not a crest, and then splaying open under the keel
and racing with the bow, the legend broke water
and was reborn, her screams of joy
and my heart drumming harder, and the pale blue islands
were no longer phantom outlines, and the elate spray
slapped our faces with joy, and everything came
back as it was between the other islets, but
those with our own names, sometimes a fin

shot up, sometimes a back arched and re-entered
the racily running waves under which they glanced;
I saw their wet brown bodies gunning seaward,
more brown than golden despite the name "dorado,"
but I guess in the wet light their skins shone
too raw, too quiet to be miraculous,
too strange to quiet my fear, the skittering fish
from the first line of the open page, held
and held until the school was lost, the prodigal's home
was the horizon while my own peaks
loomed so inconsolably again, the roads, the roofs
of Soufrière in the wet sunlight. I watched them come.

IV

I had gaped in anticipation of an emblem
carved at a fountain's pediment from another sea
and when the dolphins showed up and I saw them
they arched the way thoughts rise from memory.
They shot out of the glacial swell like skiers
hurtling themselves out of that Alpine surf
with its own crests and plungings, spuming slopes
from which the dolphins seraphically soared
to the harps of ringing wires and humming ropes
to which my heart clung and those finished hopes
that I would see you again, my twin, "my dolphin."
And yet elation drove the dolphins' course
as if both from and to you, their joy was ours.

And had there been a prophecy that said: "Wait!
On a day of great delight you will see dolphins."
Or, in the ashes and embers of a wrecked sunset
the same voice, falling as quietly as a flag, said,
before the constellations arranged their chaos,
"Those drifting cinders are angels, see how they soar,"
I would not have believed in them, being too old
and sceptical from the fury of one life's
determined benedictions, but they are here.
Angels and dolphins. The second, first.
And always certainly, steadily, on the bright rim
of the world, getting no nearer or nearer, the more
the bow's wedge shuddered towards it, prodigal,
that line of light that shines from the other shore.